Contents

Prologue

A UK Locum Physician's Starter Guide is a concise collection of my overall experience as a locum medical and respiratory registrar for fellow colleagues who are contemplating a short-term locum post or a more permanent opportunity.

Like many others at the beginning of their locum career, I wasn't able to find good comprehensive information so this is an attempt to clearly outline the overall process.

Although I'm currently in a respiratory training programme, I've accrued five months of external locum registrar experience from two very distinct hospitals, one in England and the other in Scotland. This is in addition to what was essentially one year's experience of being an internal locum medical registrar where I managed to negotiate my hourly rate above that of more senior trainees.

This guide will detail my thoughts on the difference between working in Scottish and English hospitals, locuming internally versus externally and locuming on call or during sociable hours. It'll also hopefully walk you through the process of finding a good accountant and reliable locum agency.

Reasons to locum

The first question you should ask yourself is why you want to become a locum doctor. Common reasons include greater flexibility compared to a fixed substantive post, desire for experiencing other specialties and higher pay. Let's look at all three in turn.

I have to say flexibility was probably the best part of being a locum doctor for me. During my initial three months of external agency locum work I was able to completely avoid a set of night shifts despite being on the full medical registrar rota simply by letting the rota coordinator know I was unavailable. Having never known of this luxury before, the feeling of control over your life and career is amazing.

Though it almost goes without saying that if you've signed up for a job with on-call commitments you shouldn't pull this trick often as you risk annoying both your agency and the hospital but as this is one of the few perks of being a locum doctor you'd be doing yourself a disservice if you didn't take it. Remember to give plenty of notice (a couple of weeks) if you decide to take any on call shifts off, in the interests of patient safety so the hospital can find a substitute.

Interestingly enough, I've been reliably informed by three locum agencies that only one week's notice needs to be given when requesting "annual leave" or when quitting. Initially I was concerned how the hospitals would find a replacement so soon so I ended up giving three week's advance notice for both external agency posts. To my surprise both rota coordinators and the agency did not ask a single question and the process was seamless. For someone who had worked for four years straight after graduation in consecutive substantive posts I finally discovered the power of flexibility. This also works with study leave but just ensure that the ward and department are adequately staffed.

On a slightly darker note, this flexibility can also work against you. My first external agency post was a three month opportunity, advertised as **most likely** extending to six months. My locum agency was also kept in the dark until the last two weeks when I had to firmly ask for an answer to job plan. The hospital informed me that the department didn't require me anymore and therefore would not be extending my contract to six months. Thankfully the locum doctor market is nearly always undersaturated so I found an even more attractive placement a few days later.

Just remember that although working as a locum doctor gives you flexibility to take annual leave or change jobs within one week's notice, it also allows hospitals the flexibility of giving you very little notice when a department doesn't need you anymore. The learning point is to always have plan B in case your current contract collapses.

Locuming can also give you exposure to a variety of specialties that you might not encounter during your in-programme training. After foundation, core or even specialty training you may find that you lack experience in some specialties. Some things just cannot be learned from books. For example, most doctors have an idea what medical thoracoscopy is but unless you spend an afternoon in the endoscopy suite you'll only have an abstract textbook idea of the procedure. Explaining the procedure to your patient will be very difficult and patients can tell instantly when their doctor isn't confident.

Many senior registrars and consultants recall their senior house officer years when they spent three or even four years experiencing nearly all the major medical specialties before entering higher specialty training. This is in stark contrast to the standard two years nowadays. If you find your foundation or core training programme lacking in renal medicine for example, a three month locum post will undoubtedly fix that.

As a medical registrar who had not done a renal medicine placement during core medical training, I'm finding myself reading textbooks on renal physiology again. The acute medical unit I lead during evenings and nights are staffed mainly by renal physicians so a very brief grilling is all that's required to expose the gaps in my knowledge! By locuming in new specialties you can become a much better physician fast.

And finally, whilst it's a common misconception that all locum doctors get paid £1,000s for working one weekend, it's true that locum doctors get paid better than their trainee or substantive counterparts. The media love to exaggerate how much locum doctors get remunerated as it sells newspaper but few people consider the reality. Plumbers and boiler engineers can get paid up to hundreds of pounds per hour, several-fold more than the most expensive locum doctors. If a water pipe bursts in your home and your plumber decides to charge you £1,000 for three hours of his time you don't really have a choice.

If you google "locum doctor", the first page currently contains an article about a doctor who was paid £11,000 to work one weekend. Even if it was 72 hours on-call (including at home) that still works out to be £152 an hour which is out of this world. Let's discount this example in favour of more realistic examples in a later section.

The advantages of higher pay have to be considered amongst the disadvantages of lack of holiday pay (which is why annual leave was in quotations earlier), study leave and pensions. Another important consideration is that locum work can be inconsistent if you don't play your cards right. Working as an ad-hoc locum can mean working 7 days in a row some weeks whilst other weeks there may not be any opportunities.

Reasons not to locum - Holidays, Sickness & Pensions

As a group doctors rarely take sick days. Everyone I'm working with at the moment is coughing but they continue to plod on which is very respectable. The only minor illness that should result in a sick day is really diarrhoea and vomiting for infection control reasons.

A couple of days here or there for a bad bout of flu is sometimes unavoidable but I haven't taken a single sick day in the almost five years since I graduated. Not having sick pay is often quoted to be a disadvantage when working as a locum doctor but in my opinion it's negligible. This obviously doesn't apply if you're struck by a terrible diagnosis or involved in an accident but I guess that's what insurance is for.

On the other hand, I found the lack of holiday pay and study leave a significant disadvantage. Not being paid on bank holidays or any annual leave can be worrying if you're paid hourly. When you work substantively, your pay and your rota doesn't tend to vary dramatically but as a locum, taking a couple weeks annual leave can leave you struggling financially and with guilt if you don't plan accordingly.

As a result you should plan a few months in advance ensuring you have consistent work. Invest in a good calendar (or electronic one) and mark the days where you'll be off (weekends, bank holidays and annual leave) and ensure that your salary from the days you work cover your expenses. If it doesn't then you'll have to take on a few more shifts here or there in the lead up to your holidays. Don't leave these things until the last minute because worrying about finances is the last thing you need as a doctor. Instead of ruminating about money we need to continue learning and developing to become better physicians.

No study leave was personally very limiting. In contrast, during core medical training I worked in a hospital that offered 30 days of study leave per year. I was studying for MRCP at the time so actually used a good portion of it for private study, exam days and courses. Not having to worry about working extra shifts to cover for a lost day of work was very invaluable now that I look back. This is often an understated advantage of being a substantive trainee and in addition to MRCP, allowed me to take days off to obtain competencies (for example, central line insertion course).

This wouldn't have been realistic to achieve during my locum months as not only would I be missing work and not getting paid, I'd also have to pay for expensive courses, accommodation and travel expenses. Not being able to attend courses for CPD was something that made me feel quite guilty as I felt I was letting my patients down.

The other major disadvantage often discussed is not being able to contribute to a NHS pension but I would strongly disagree. Although it is outwith the scope of this book to discuss self invested personal pensions (SIPP), a continuous infusion of money into your SIPP can easily be made monthly with the help of a good accountant.

Although SIPP contributions are tax deductible, you still need money for living expenses so ensure you don't get too carried away and over-contribute even though the tax relief can seem quite generous. The money you contribute will sit there (either as cash or investments of your choosing) and cannot be withdrawn or used until your minimum pension age. This is currently 55 but will increase to 57 in 2028. Also be aware that the government changes pension rules very often so I wouldn't recommend being too over-enthusiastic with a SIPP but the option is always there for you to experiment.

As you can see, although the higher rates of pay initially look quite attractive, lack of holiday pay, study leave and the NHS pension brings the two salaries a lot closer together. I still feel that external agency locums have the edge but as always, do your own research and speak to other locum doctors before making any decisions.

What Type Of Locum Should I Be?

If I haven't discouraged you yet (!) then this is the next question you should ask yourself. You can choose between internal or external locum work; on-call rotas or just 0900 - 1700 only; sporadic shifts or longer term posts spanning three months or even longer.

Internal locum work is good for doctors who already have a training or substantive post and are looking to make some extra money or gain some more experience on top of their "base" job.

The rates are usually slightly lower than external locum rates but you have the advantage of the hospital payroll remunerating you through their pay-as-you-earn (PAYE) system saving you the hassle of finding an accountant or filing your own tax returns. You can find internal locum work by contacting your rota coordinator, who will normally give you an invaluable first refusal on available shifts. The main advantage that stands out is the familiarity you'll have with your own hospital environment, including the staff and the hospital IT systems.

I worked as an internal locum registrar during my core medical training and found this an extremely good way to gain registrar experience and earn some extra money to pay for MRCP courses. The number of shifts I could take were very limited due to a busy CMT on call rota so it's not the most effective way of earning money. An internal locum can also be referred to as bank staff.

There's another way you can successfully work as an internal locum doctor and I've seen several colleagues pull this off. Say you've completed a training programme or a substantive post and for the next six months you want to take a career break. You can ask your rota coordinator from the hospital you've just left whether they'll keep you in their internal bank of staff. Everything is as above with the added option of doing as many shifts as you like if the demand is there.

Alternatively you can work as an external locum doctor via an agency for which I personally found the rates to be slightly (10-20%) higher. When you first register with locum agencies there's a list of paperwork to assemble. With the change in rules on limited companies, it's probably best to consult a professional consultant about working through an umbrella company. For a small weekly fee, they'll offer you their advice and process your payroll, deducting the necessary tax. This will save you the hassle of filling in paperwork and leave you more time to spend with your family.

In return for your extra efforts in becoming an external locum, you'll expose yourself to the wider UK locum doctor market. After signing up to three locum agencies I consistently received offers numerous times per week spanning Scotland, England and Wales. This is undoubtedly the best way to ensure you never run out of work.

The next decision to make is whether you want to work on-call or just 0900 - 1700 only. Some posts are 0900 to 1700 only with the majority having some element of on call work. Working on-call can certainly be very rewarding in terms of finances and experience, simply because you're working more hours. If you're working as a senior house officer with a couple layers of seniority (safety) above you then there's not as much concern working out of hour shifts at a completely new hospital. If anything goes wrong, you can always keep calm and bleep the med reg as they say.

However, if you're planning to do on call work as a medical registrar or consultant then I'd strongly advise familiarising yourself with the hospital system first. This includes the hospital layout in the event of emergencies and also the IT system. Ensure your first couple of weeks are 0900 - 1700 with plenty of substantive staff around to point you in the right direction. Also ensure that you have all the relevant usernames, passwords and access to wards before you work evenings, weekends and nights.

Looking back at the times when I found locum doctors unhelpful and actually a drag on team performance, most of the time it was just lack of preparation or effort. Many would turn up for a night shift with little to no prior experience of the hospital system and frustratingly no usernames, passwords or prior training to the computer systems. It was often faster on a busy night shift to request blood tests and clerk patients myself rather than spend time teaching them. This is especially true when temporary staff are only covering for one or two isolated shifts. There's a stigma attached to locum doctors being less able but the reality is that being in a completely new environment reduces your efficiency many-fold.

If you have the option I'd strongly recommend having a detailed discussion with the departmental consultants and the rota coordinator regarding what I call a phased locum post. If the post is three months, ensure that your first two weeks are only 0900 - 1700 where most substantive staff are available. For the next couple of weeks, start adding in evenings and weekends where there's still a basic level of staff around. Once you're confident with ward work and on call work for your new hospital then you can start considering night shifts. This prioritises patient safety but also helps you to strike up good first impressions with your colleagues.

Because lack of preparation makes on-call locum work potentially dangerous for you and your patients, only working 0900 - 1700 understandably looks quite attractive. The two months I worked "off-call" was probably the most pleasant part of my career so far. I owned all my evenings and weekends and had no more sleepless nights due to not having to work any of them!

This is also outwith the scope of this book but I now realise that the reason it was so pleasant was because I was well inside my comfort zone and did not develop as a doctor during those two months. In hindsight, short periods (<3 months) of 0900 - 1700 are acceptable but longer periods could leave us deskilled, less confident and stagnant.

So much we learn is from running around like "headless chickens", as nurses say, seeing patient after patient after patient. Without that urgency, 0900 - 1700 becomes one big ward round or clinic with very little intellectual stimulation.

Although I enjoyed every weekend off during those two months, the last few weeks of work were soul destroying. It consisted of morning ward round, jobs, lunch followed by more jobs. I made little progress as a registrar except for the few pleural procedures I did on the ward. If you're planning on taking up a 0900 - 1700 long term post then I would advise adding in a few on-call shifts just to stop yourself from going rusty.

Decide on your grade

At first, this seems an odd comment to make but the decision really depends on your confidence and career approach.

For example, if you've recently completed core training or higher specialty training then you may want some more experience at that level before advancing to registrar or consultant level respectively. This is mainly for two reasons - the first and most important is patient safety. As a medical registrar you'll be expected to lead cardiac arrests and make some very difficult decisions on-call and if you've never had any registrar experience during your core training, then working as a locum registrar right off the bat may not be the best option. This particularly rings true if you've decided to locum at a completely new hospital.

I became an internal locum medical registrar "overnight" at the end of CT1 but this was on the background of knowing my hospital inside out and being acquainted with most of my colleagues and consultants. All the consultants were confident in my ability so this boosted my confidence. I also knew I had approachable people including the second medical registrar to seek help from if required.

When deciding on the grade you wish to work at, I would base my decision on my own level of confidence, amount of clinical experience and also environmental factors such as whether there is on site support (e.g. second medical registrar if you're planning to act up as a med reg).

Negotiate Your Hourly Rate Despite The Locum Price Cap

Hospitals generally set "fixed" internal rates. The English hospital I core medically trained in paid £26/hour for foundation year 1 doctors, £35 or £42/hour for senior house officers and £43 or £52 for registrars, depending on social or unsocial hours. The current Scottish hospital I'm working for only pays £26/hour for registrar shifts so there is a significant variation.

During CT1/CT2 I was working some internal locum medical registrar shifts on top of my busy rota. The shifts ended up being really stressful and I felt the hourly rate didn't compensate me appropriately, especially for the sleep and social time I was sacrificing. My initial plan was to reduce the number of extra shifts I was taking on and just obtain some med reg experience. However, one day I asked the rota coordinator whether my hourly rates could be increased to £65/hour, fully expecting a refusal as this was a higher rate than what the "proper" registrars themselves were receiving.

To my surprise, she sought approval from the hospital finance department immediately and the rest was history. My argument at the time was that agency staff were getting paid more than the headline internal rate for doing the same job. With their unfamiliarity with our hospital, the standard of care had to be lower than mine and therefore I was able to negotiate the higher rate. Don't be afraid to ask for a higher rate even if you're only an SHO doing a registrar's job, especially if your hospital is requesting a last minute shift. As long as you're doing the job well, there's no reason you should be paid less just because you're junior. Doctors' personal time is already very precious so any extra hours dedicated to providing a good service undoubtedly deserves a premium rate.

As an external locum doctor you need to set your own rate. It all comes down to supply and demand. Working as the medical registrar at my training hospital was very demanding and had lots of responsibility. In addition, they were understaffed at registrar level so there was an opportunity to ask for a higher rate. They ended up paying more than £65/hour to external agency doctors anyway so they were saving money.

For senior house officer level I would aim for a range between £35 - £45/hour before tax. I know a couple of SHO doctors who earned £50/hour but they were almost registrar level and had the benefit of knowing the hospitals inside out and were also willing to relocate. For registrar level I would aim between £55 - £85/hour. Most of the locum registrars I came across earned £60 - £70/hour and I fell in the same category during my five months of external work.

For consultant level I would aim between £80 - £110/hour. I knew some consultants on just £65/hour but there were a couple earning £120+/hour for odd shifts.

The above is a very rough guide and will vary significantly depending on your circumstances. It goes without saying that if you're willing to relocate the above rates could potentially be surpassed. For example, I have received offers of £85/hour and even £110/hour as a medical registrar but simply could not afford to move across the country at the time.

The general rule is don't undersell yourself because locum agencies will pay you the lowest rate you'll accept. If you request £50/hour there's no chance of getting paid £51/hour.

Understandably, agencies wish to confirm your reliability as a doctor who has good relationships with patients, colleagues and hospitals. When you start your career as a locum physician, be willing to accept jobs that pay slightly less than you expect.

For instance, as a SHO, accept a job that pays £35/hour for a couple of months to strengthen your relationship with the agency before asking for £40 - £45. As a registrar, work for a respectable £55/hour before building towards £80/hour if possible.

Just a note about the locum rates cap - from April 2016 all medical staff working for locum agencies are theoretically bound by the government cap of +55%. If your standard hourly rate is £20 that means the maximum hourly rate you can theoretically achieve is £31. The logistics of this price cap varies depending on the geographical area and if you establish a good relationship with your agency they can point you in the right direction.

Realistically no medical registrar (or even SHO) would be willing to work for £31/hour for such a demanding and sometimes thankless job. Thankfully the locum cap has been overridden on many occasions simply based on supply and demand and will continue to be in the interests of patient safety. Speaking for myself as a respiratory registrar, I would choose to work as a locum SHO with a lot less stress if the rates are that low before 40% tax.

Timing

If you're currently looking for a locum post then I would immediately put this book down and contact the locum agencies now!

However, if you're in a training or substantive post and have a finish date in mind, when should you contact them? From experience, all the locum agencies I've worked with respond within 24 hours by email or within a few hours on the phone. It's slightly different out of hours but there's still normally a point of contact.

The mistake I made was contacting them a bit too soon. My core medical training was coming to an end at the start of August but being quite organised I contacted three agencies at the start of May. After assimilating all the requested documents and attending the "interviews" I was bombarded by countless job offers on a daily basis. Towards the last couple of weeks I came across a job with the perfect location, specialty and hourly rate so immediately accepted the position.

In hindsight although it may have coincided with the changeover in August but had I left all the registration and logistical work including mandatory e-learning until July I think someone else would've been offered that position first.

Even if you're currently in a training programme with a few months before completion date I'd strongly recommend registering with three locum agencies. Occupational health and references can take some time to collect as you're relying on other people. In the event you've completed registration before you're available for jobs, there's no harm in turning down jobs before your ideal opportunity appears. Hospitals are usually quite understanding so if your start date needs delayed by several days (personal reasons or changeover) then they frequently accommodate this.

Contact Locum Agencies

After you've decided on your grade and hourly rate you might wish to contact locum agencies. You generally want to apply for three agencies just to cover geographical area and gain experience with interacting with different ones. Apply for more than three and you become overwhelmed with paperwork. Less than three and you may not be able to differentiate between a locum agency that looks after you from one that doesn't.

You can decide to fill in an online form on their website, email them or call them directly. I emailed them using the same template stating my conditions for efficiency.

Dear Agency,

I'm a respiratory and medical registrar currently available for a long term locum post between April 2017 and July 2017. I'm seeking an hourly rate of £60/hour, am willing to relocate but will need hospital accommodation.

Attached is my CV, thanks.

Kind regards,
Rory

The agencies I'm currently registered with are:

Medacs
HCL Doctors
ID Medical

If after reading this book you decide to register with any of them most agencies promote a referral system where both of us receive some free beer money after you've done some shifts with them. It doesn't impact on your hourly rate so if you mention you were referred by me I'd be very grateful. Plus it's extra beer for you too!

To make you more attractive to hospitals, the locum agencies will need an up-to-date CV so make sure that this is the first thing they have from you. If you include this in your opening email then this will save time and demonstrate to them that you're reliable and organised.

What I discovered is that each locum agency seems to have their own "territory" when supplying staff to the hospitals. For example Scotland predominantly uses Medacs whilst HCL is much more prevalent in the Yorkshire and Humber area.

After registration, they'll either send you ad-hoc shifts or longer term posts, depending on your stated preference. You may decide to work ad-hoc locum shifts with all the agencies you register with. For me, I ended up only working through Medacs for both of my locum posts as I prefer building good relationships.

Locum agencies generally earn a rate for every hour you work and therefore they'll prefer someone who is looking for a long term locum post. For every hour I worked they earned around £4 which is quite significant over a five month full time period. The stories you hear in the media are generally exaggerated and I suspect that unless you're earning way below my above guidance then the agencies don't make the inflated figures we see in newspapers.

Each locum agency you register with will assign a candidate officer to you who "looks after" you during your post so if you have any doubts, don't be afraid to ask for help or transparency. Ask how much they make for every hour you work and if the answer is suspicious then simply move on. The locum market is very undersaturated so your options are plentiful.

Find a good accountant

Whilst the option exists to submit your own tax returns, the number of hours spent researching how to do this and then actually performing the task means it's probably not worth your time. Using that time for an extra couple of shifts would easily pay for a good accountant.

Since the new rules, working under your own limited company is no longer an option. Even if it were still an option, the government's new dividend allowance renders a limited company essentially pointless.

The main option, I've been informed, is opening an umbrella company that's managed by your accountant for a small weekly fee in the region of £10. Your accountant would then process your payslip and pay the necessary national insurance and tax before paying you the remaining balance. A good accountant will also have your best interests at heart and offer to claim certain eligible business expenses through the company further reducing your tax bill.

There are accountancy firms that specifically tailor to contractors. I would advocate initially reading through their websites to properly understand the services that they can offer. This should then be followed up by a direct phone call to the accountant who would be working with you. Using this strategy will ensure no communication issues.

Personally I used an experienced firm called Bradleys Accountants. They were fantastic, reliable and still help me with advice till this day. They also have a referral bonus scheme so if you decide to use their services I'd be grateful if you say I referred you as both of us will get rewarded.

Checklist of items you need to bring

After you've sent the locum agencies an email with your CV they'll request a list of documents which can be slightly overwhelming at first.

<u>Immediate</u>

Up to date CV
References (minimum 2)
Disclosure and Barring Service (DBS) or equivalent
Occupational Health

<u>Other</u>

Proof of address (two, to support DBS check)
Passport and driving license
Basic and Higher Qualifications
GMC certificate and/or annual retention letter
Health Declaration
Registration

The list has been separated into two lists to highlight the difference in urgency. After submitting your CV, you should make immediate contact with two referees (consultants who have worked with you) and occupational health. The usual information including vaccinations and viral titres should be requested as proof and if required you may need booster vaccinations. Remember that blood tests screening for blood borne viruses must be documented as an identified validated sample (IVS), otherwise it may be invalid. The last major item to request immediately is a disclosure and barring service (DBS) check or equivalent as it often takes weeks to clear.

The rest of the documents shown above are relatively self-explanatory. Proof of address can be utility or council tax bills. Locating your medical degree certificate, MRCP/MRCS certificates and any other relevant degrees should be a priority. If you don't have a GMC certificate, locum agencies frequently accept the annual retention letter. You can find this by logging onto GMC online, clicking onto My Account followed by Documents.

"Interview" and Learning Modules

After confirming your eligibility to work as a locum, agencies will ask for a face-to-face "interview". From my experience of attending two interviews the first reason is to confirm the original copies of your passport and medical degrees.

Secondly the agency must ensure you have good communication skills with a sound grasp of English. They have a reputation to maintain with the hospitals and a series of unsuitable locum doctors could potentially blacklist a locum agency.

For the interview dress like you would for work. It's not a true interview so I wouldn't waste time in preparation - they only test your basic communication skills. Included at the end were a couple of learning modules on fire safety and safe lifting, although the latter was more directed towards nurses.

Both agencies also had a very long list of e-learning modules that we had to complete in our own personal time. Modules including working with adults or children, fire safety and common medical law like competency and ethics. I would recommend completing these as soon as possible so that the locum agencies can start looking for opportunities ASAP.

Picking the right job

If you have a family with young children, working away from home for months on end isn't a viable option even if the hourly rate was £300/hour. Your choice of jobs are more limited and consequently your negotiable rate may drop. However, if your other half can look after the young ones, traveling further away and returning every weekend is an option. In the end, not having to relocate long distances has obvious advantages such as not having to seek accommodation or having to learn an entirely foreign hospital system.

If you're young or single then it might be worthwhile to move a few hundred miles in the search for a new experience. As compensation for your inconvenience, higher rates can be negotiated but the downside of course is that relocation and accommodation expenses will have to be factored in.

The first thing when choosing a job is to ensure accommodation is available, whether that's your own house, hospital accommodation or a rented apartment. Secondly, look at your own professional needs. If you're an experienced consultant looking for flexibility and a higher rate of pay then picking the perfect specialty is less of a concern. For example gastroenterologists and respiratory physicians who are maybe winding down towards retirement may choose to work in the acute medicine unit if they're dual accredited. On the other hand, picking the "correct" specialty is of utmost importance for senior house officers.

After accommodation and specialty, the third main consideration should be the rate of pay. Refer back to the chapter on how to decide your own rate and learn to negotiate. Always request more than you're willing to accept and expect locum agencies and hospitals to haggle your price down!

The Rota Coordinator Is Your Best Friend

One of the most important people to become acquainted with immediately is the rota coordinator. Their knowledge of rota gaps is second to none. Even when they don't have the answer they can refer you to someone who does.

The reason why you must introduce yourself to the rota coordinator **before** you start your post is because agencies often have little clue where you should report to on your first day. You'll find that your goals are almost completely aligned with those of the rota coordinator's - by settling in seamlessly you make their job infinitely easier! If you quit after the first day as a consequence of their poor communication or organisation then they'll have to look for another doctor all over again.

Ask for the on-call rota (if you're on call), the wards and departments you'll be expected to work in and also the departmental consultants' emails. Ask to be included in their email list for any rota or news updates. Note that some rota coordinators prefer to use mobile phones instead. Nurturing a positive relationship means that eventually you'll have the first refusal on extra shifts and can also negotiate better rates once you've become familiar with the hospital system.

Ask for an induction

Having worked in a reasonable number of hospitals spanning Scotland and England, the variation is incredible even within the same specialty.

One English hospital had six respiratory registrars and because I was acting up as one (and therefore the most junior) I was consistently placed on the in-reach team where I had plenty of experience seeing referrals, doing clinics and numerous pleural procedures. I must've placed at least 20 chest drains in those 2 months.

In another Scottish hospital I was the only respiratory registrar. I placed two chest drains over the two months but was otherwise supernumerary. The consultants were entirely self sufficient - they did their own pleural procedures, saw their own referrals and even wrote their own ward round notes!

Another English hospital had three respiratory registrars and it was a mix of the above two hospitals. I felt mostly supernumerary but essentially managed a ward with some juniors. This hospital used 7 different IT systems - one for blood test results, one for X-rays, one for ordering investigations, two for looking at old clinical letters, one for electronic prescriptions and one for palliative care documents.

As you can hopefully appreciate, there is some merit in spending a day familiarising yourself to the hospital and the IT systems. The last hospital I mentioned held an 8-hour IT induction. Even if you understand the IT systems, it's always worth attending these to obtain usernames, passwords and a trust email account.

Introspection & Long Term Locuming

I wanted to end this guide by discussing the concept of long term locum work.

There are reasons why locum doctors have a bad reputation inside and outside of the NHS. Apart from annual appraisals and five yearly revalidation, locums aren't required to maintain eportfolio commitments and therefore the urgency to maintain professional development is simply not there. Some of the tickboxes like obtaining central line experience in core medical training are quite tricky but because it's mandatory, the vast majority of us obtain it. Not having anything mandatory is nice but is a double edged sword when it comes to maintenance of our skills and keeping up with our peers.

Locum doctors also have different objectives and may be more entrepreneur minded. They may move around the country much more often and therefore have many more distractions like accountancy work, estate agencies and admin work when compared to the "normal" doctor.

However, as locums, we need to have some introspection and sense of responsibility and duty towards our patients. We need to remember that we are accountable for every action and prescription we make. At the end of the day, we aren't entrepreneurs and should automate as much of the non-clinical work as possible. Consider working an extra shift to pay for that good accountant instead of performing the work yourself. Live close to the hospital so that saved hour can be used to sleep or catch up on some reading. If your loved one works part time or stays at home, consider asking them to help you find accommodation or negotiate with locum agencies.

Use the time saved to learn something new every day so that you can become a better doctor. I suppose it's slightly easier as a registrar or a consultant as you only need to know a lot about a little but read a few pages of a medical book or half a journal article every day.

When you become a better doctor, your patients will have more trust in you and in turn you'll have more job satisfaction. When you become a better doctor, you'll automatically receive better opportunities and rates from agencies. In turn you can offer to spend less time searching for these jobs and more time becoming a better doctor.

When you become a better doctor, your colleagues will respect you more and together we can start challenging the notion that "most locum doctors are rubbish". Remember that without respect your job becomes an uphill struggle every day. Request high quality work from others but request the highest quality from yourself.

Printed in Great Britain
by Amazon